groove

THE BASICS

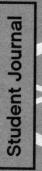

GROOVE: THE BASICS

Groove is published by Youth Ministry Partners and Abingdon Press, The United Methodist Publishing House, 2222 Rosa L. Parks Blvd., P.O. Box 280988, Nashville, TN 37228-0988. Copyright © 2015 Youth Ministry Partners and Abingdon Press.

Scripture quotations unless noted otherwise are from the Common English Bible. Copyright © 2011 by the Common English Bible. All rights reserved. Used by permission. (*CommonEnglishBible.com*)

Groove Team

Neil M. Alexander: Publisher
Marjorie M. Pon: Editor, Church School Publications
Jack Radcliffe: Managing Editor
Jason Sansbury: Editor
Sheila K. Hewitt: Production Editing Supervisor
Pam Shepherd: Production Editor
Keely Moore: Design Manager
Kellie Green: Designer
Michael Adkins: Writer
Zach Moffatt: Devotional Writer

15 16 17 18 19 20 21 22 23 24 — 10 9 8 7 6 5 4 3 2 1

Contents

Welcome

Welcome to *Groove: The Basics!* You have in your hands the *Groove: The Basics Student Journal*. You may be wondering, "What is this thing called a student journal?" It is a book designed to assist you as you explore, enjoy, engage in, wrestle with, and reflect on all that you experience over the next four weeks with your friends. It's your place to be creative and honest.

This student journal is a place to track your thoughts and ideas during the large group learning time. You can follow the highlights from the teaching through the prompts provided, and there's space to take it in a new direction.

Devotions: *Devotion* is a long word that means one simple thing: a short time of worship. Each week you will look at who God created you to become. There are five brief times of worship during which you will think and pray about what God is saying and what it means for your life. You choose when during the week, where, and how you want to spend these times. There is no special formula to these devotions, so use them however works best for you.

You'll need a Bible (printed or electronic version) and a pen or pencil for writing and drawing. We recommend the Contemporary English Bible (CEB). If you don't have a Bible, talk with your youth leader or download it on your smartphone or tablet by using an app such as YouVersion, created by LifeChurch.tv, or download the free CEB or other versions of your choice. You'll need to download the Bible within the app so that you won't need Internet access or Wi-Fi to read your Bible on your device.

Each devotion comes with a few questions and space to reflect on what God is doing in your life. They end with a short prayer or a prayer focus statement. Feel free to use what's provided or talk with God anyway you'd like.

Enjoy the *Groove* experience!

The Trinity

Look Up
Matthew 3:13-17

[13]*At that time Jesus came from Galilee to the Jordan River so that John would baptize him.* [14]*John tried to stop him and said, "I need to be baptized by you, yet you come to me?"*

[15]*Jesus answered, "Allow me to be baptized now. This is necessary to fulfill all righteousness."*

So John agreed to baptize Jesus. [16]*When Jesus was baptized, he immediately came up out of the water. Heaven was opened to him, and he saw the Spirit of God coming down like a dove and resting on him.* [17]*A voice from heaven said, "This is my Son whom I dearly love; I find happiness in him."*

"Bring me a worm that can comprehend a man, and then I will show you a man that can comprehend the Triune God."—John Wesley

Look Up

"Tri" (means _____) +

"Unitas" (means _____)

= Trinity

Sum Up

- *Which piece of the Trinity do you feel you know the least about?*

- *Why do you think that is?*

- *How can you address the knowledge gap?*

Wrap Up

Take some time to thank each person of the Trinity for something specific in your life and faith.

God the Father

Jesus the Son

The Holy Spirit

Lace Them Up

Complete this sentence:

Because of what I have heard and read today, I have learned . . .

Coming Up

Answer this question:

- *What is the Gospel?*

The Word Became Flesh

Read John 1:1-5.

What exactly is the Trinity? Christians have asked this question for more than 2,000 years. The Trinity is the idea that God is three persons in one being. We have God the Father, God the Son, and God the Holy Spirit. They are not fully separate beings but are related and are involved with one another in everything they do. They are joined together in an eternal dance of love.

Write on page 15 how you imagine the Trinity, based on this Scripture. Draw; sketch; write a poem. Get creative, because our Triune God is definitely creative.

Prayer: God, I know that I am not meant to fully understand how you operate. I am not meant to understand how you work as a Triune God. But I do understand how much you love your creation; and for that, I am forever grateful. Amen.

Journal Page

Day 2

God the Father/Creator

Read Genesis 1:1-5.

Use the space provided to reflect on the following questions:

- *How does this reflect the Trinity?*
- *How, do you think, were the Son and the Spirit involved in creation?*
- *When and how do we experience God as Creator?*

When God created the universe, God said that everything was good. The earth was good, the light was good, the water was good, and humanity was good. Everything was good. This means that we are good. Sometimes we just forget that.

- *What does it mean that we are created in the image of God, the Trinity?*

Prayer: Holy Creator, we thank you for creating us in your image. Thank you for creating today and waking us up to experience today. Help us always do what you created us to do, which is love. Amen.

Journal Page

God the Son

Read Matthew 1:23.

Think about all that you know about the Christmas story. Draw a line across the middle of page 19 and a line down the middle from the top down to that line, making two sections on top and one on the bottom.

- On the top left side, write whatever comes to mind when you think about the birth of Jesus.
- On the top right side, write whatever comes to mind when you think about the life of Jesus.
- On the bottom, write whatever comes to mind when you think about Jesus Christ's death on the cross.

Read Luke 23:46-49.

- *What is significant about the idea of God dying on the cross?*

Reflect on what it means for us that Jesus, the second part of the Trinity, was Emanuel or "God With Us."

Prayer: Blessed Trinity, you understand human pain and human joy. Help me always rely on you. Help me always seek out your comfort. Amen.

Journal Page

God the Spirit

Read Acts 2:1-3.

The Holy Spirit is third part of the Godhead sent by Jesus to empower his followers to be his witnesses.

Reflect on the image that stood out to you the most. Write or draw that image. As you do this, think about what the Holy Spirit is trying to tell you through this story.

- *Why, do you think, does Luke, the writer of Acts, describe God's activity that day as a rush of violent wind?*
- *What does that imagery tell us about God?*

Prayer: Holy God, fill me with your Holy Spirit. Allow your winds of love to move me and guide me. Allow the fire in my heart to be ignited for your glory, and let it spark a passion in me for justice and grace. Amen.

Journal Page

Day 5

Silence

Read 1 Kings 19:11-13 slowly. As you read through it the first time, pick out the word or phrase that means the most to you. As you read through it the second time, think of moments in your life that were as violent as the rushing winds, as devastating as the tremendous earthquake, or as vicious as the fire. Think about what you did during those moments. Read through the passage a third time. This time, focus on where God was.

In your journal, reflect on a moment when life was so loud that you had no idea which way to turn. What did you do? Whom did you talk to? How did God encounter you?

Prayer: Creator, Redeemer, Sustainer, allow me to be still each day of my life and truly know that you are God. Amen.

Journal Page

The Gospel and Scripture

Look Up
2 Timothy 3:14-17

> [14]*But you must continue with the things you have learned and found convincing. You know who taught you.* [15]*Since childhood you have known the holy scriptures that help you to be wise in a way that leads to salvation through faith that is in Christ Jesus.* [16]*Every scripture is inspired by God and is useful for teaching, for showing mistakes, for correcting, and for training character,* [17]*so that the person who belongs to God can be equipped to do everything that is good.*

Romans 6:16

¹⁶Don't you know that if you offer yourselves to someone as obedient slaves, that you are slaves of the one whom you obey? That's true whether you serve as slaves of sin, which leads to death, or as slaves of the kind of obedience that leads to righteousness.

Sum Up

All Scripture is _____ by God.

Scripture is meant to _____ us.

Scripture points us toward _____.

We can either _____ sin, or be

_____ sin.

Wrap Up

- *How might the Scriptures equip us, much like the bats and gloves equip baseball players?*

- *In your own words: Why is the crucifixion and resurrection of Jesus significant to the world?*

- *How is his crucifixion and resurrection significant to you?*

Lace Them Up

Complete this sentence:

My goal for Bible reading this week is . . .

Coming Up

Answer this question:

- *What is the church?*

Their Story Is Our Story

Read 2 Timothy 3:14-16.

Paul is reminding Timothy to always rely upon God's Word, for it is holy and powerful.

Use the space provided to reflect on the following questions:

- *Have you ever gone through a situation that you did not know how to handle?*
- *Where did you go or whom did you talk to for guidance?*
- *If you sought God's Word for guidance, what did you do as a result of what you learned? What was the result?*
- *If you didn't seek God's Word, how might the outcome have been different if you had sought out God's Word?*

Remember, God's Word, the Bible, is not some magical book that cures all of our ailments or gets rid of our temptations. It tells the story of people who have experienced God's powerful love.

Prayer: God, help me remember that no matter what I am going through in my life, I can always find comfort in your Word. Your Word was there for your Son, Jesus, it was there for the early church, and it is here for me now. Thank you for your presence and comfort through the words your disciples wrote through your power so long ago. Amen.

Journal Page

A Lighted Path

Read Psalm 119:97-105 three times slowly. After the first time, circle a word or a phrase that stood out to you or write it down in the journaling space. After you read it for the second time, pay attention to any other words or phrases that resonated with you. As you read through this passage the third time, reflect on this question:

- *What truth or truths is this psalm writer trying to get across?*

After you reflect on this passage, write or draw the truth you received from this psalm.

- *How have you experienced God's Word lighting the path of your life?*

Prayer Focus: Talk to God about how God wants you to live. Are you living according to God's Word and will? Are you going through a time of turmoil and difficulty? How can God's Word light your path so that you know which way to go?

Journal Page

Day 3

Abide

Before you read the Scripture for today, think about the word *abide*. Take a few minutes and jot down what comes to mind when you hear that word. What images come to your head? What do you think of? What do you think it means?

Read John 15:1-17.

Now imagine your life if you were to fully remain in Christ.

- *What would be different?*
- *What would be the same?*

Write down some examples or draw what comes to mind.

Prayer: Holy God, help me remain in you in all that I do. It is through you that I experience true love and grace; and for that, I cannot be thankful enough. Amen.

Journal Page

Do!

Read Mark 9:1-6.

In this story, Jesus calls his twelve disciples and gives them a challenge. He challenges them to go out and spread the Gospel, the good news, to all they encounter. He told them to go, to heal, to love, to care, to sacrifice.

Brainstorm different ways that you are called to go out and spread the Gospel. As you list various ways to serve, put a star next to the most important two; and challenge yourself to do those in the next week. Whether you are helping your sibling with his or her chores, feeding our dear friends on the streets, or doing some other worthy tasks, remember that we are called to serve with our fellow brothers and sisters.

Prayer: Use the themes in Micah 6:8 as the basis for your prayer time. Ask God to show you how to do the things highlighted in the passage.

Journal Page

Hope

Read Romans 1:16-17.

Hope is one of those amazing, mysterious things within the human experience. Hope keeps people going during times of trouble.

Use the space provided to reflect on your hopes and dreams.

Paul says that we should not be ashamed of the Gospel and Scriptures of Christ. They are our story of hope that can sustain us throughout life.

Reflect on what it means for you to live by faith.

Prayer: God, thank you for the hope you promise us through your Word. As we read your stories, we see that your presence is always constant even if we don't always notice it. Help us always remember that you are with us, as your Word promises. Amen.

Journal Page

The Church

Look Up
Acts 2:42-47

[42]*The believers devoted themselves to the apostles' teaching, to the community, to their shared meals, and to their prayers.* [43]*A sense of awe came over everyone. God performed many wonders and signs through the apostles.* [44]*All the believers were united and shared everything.* [45]*They would sell pieces of property and possessions and distribute the proceeds to everyone who needed them.* [46]*Every day, they met together in the temple and ate in their homes. They shared food with gladness and simplicity.* [47]*They praised God and demonstrated God's goodness to everyone. The Lord added daily to the community those who were being saved.*

1 Corinthians 11:23-26

^{23}I received a tradition from the Lord, which I also handed on to you: on the night on which he was betrayed, the Lord Jesus took bread. ^{24}After giving thanks, he broke it and said, "This is my body, which is for you; do this to remember me." ^{25}He did the same thing with the cup, after they had eaten, saying, "This cup is the new covenant in my blood. Every time you drink it, do this to remember me." ^{26}Every time you eat this bread and drink this cup, you broadcast the death of the Lord until he comes.

Sum Up

You _____ the church, and

the church _____ you.

As a member of a church, you're there to be

support _____ and

support _____ .

Wrap Up

You learned that as a part of a church, you're not just there to be supported but also to be supportive.

- *How does your church (or the individuals that comprise it) support you?*

- *In what ways do you support your church (or the individuals that comprise it)?*

Lace Them Up

Use the space provided below to write a letter to your church. What do you praise? What would you suggest the church do differently or not at all? What should your church do that it does not?

Coming Up

- *What is the best part of life?*

Day 1

One Body

Read 1 Corinthians 12:12-31.

Use the space provided to reflect on the following questions:

- *How do you see these gifts in the people of your church?*
- *How can the church better appreciate the gifts God has given and that God's people share?*

The beautiful thing about the church is that it is a gathering of various people with a variety of skills and gifts that make up one body. With Christ as the head of our body, the church is able to be a beacon of love and light.

Prayer: God, as you lead your church, allow us to celebrate our diversity but to also recognize that we are all a part of the same body, the body of your Son. Amen.

Journal Page

Salt and Light

Read Matthew 5:13-16.

Use the space provided to answer the following questions:

- *What makes light useful?*
- *Why, do you think, did Jesus use the images of salt and light?*
- *What, do you think, does this passage say about what the character and nature of the church needs to be?*

As the church, we are called to be a shining light on a hill. We are called to stand up for what is right, to stand up for what is just, and to stand for what Jesus preached—love. As the church, we are called to love, no matter what.

As the church, we are called to be a beacon of light and hope. We are called to show the world what true love and grace look like. As you finish this devotion, reflect on whether or not you think the church is living up to this. If not, what can the church do to live up to this?

Prayer: God, allow me to love in such a way that pleases you. Amen.

Journal Page

Day 3

The People

Read Ephesians 4:1-6.

Use the space provided to list or draw what comes to your mind when you think about church.

- *What came to your mind? A building? Pews? A hymn or a song? Baptism, the Lord's Supper, stained-glassed windows?*

The church is not any of that. The church is the people. Our common trust in Christ makes us connected in ways that we will never be able to imagine. The church building, programs, and practices are important but don't define the church.

- *Based on this passage, how do you imagine the church to be?*

Rewrite Ephesians 4:1-6 in your own words in any way you'd like—an infographic (such as a chart or diagram), a word montage, a paragraph, a picture, and so on.

Prayer: Lord, allow me to be a great example of your love; and allow your Church, the people, to be a wondrous light in our darkened world. Amen.

Journal Page

Day 4

Service

Read Matthew 25:31-40.

When we see someone naked and we give them clothes or when we see someone hungry and we feed them, we are showing him or her the love and compassion that God shows us each and every day.

Use the space provided to answer the following questions:

- *What is Jesus trying to say to his followers and listeners in this story?*
- *Does your church do anything that Jesus lists here?*
- *On a scale of 1 to 10, rate how important you think mission work is for the church. Why did you rate it the way you did?*
- *What do you or your friends think when you hear the words* mission *and* service?
- *How does that line up or not line up with the model of mission work that Jesus presents us with in this passage?*

Prayer Focus: Pray for those who are on the streets, who are in prison, who are hungry, who are widowed, who are orphaned, who have no place to go. Focus your prayers on others today.

groove: The Basics

Journal Page

Do Not Be Conformed

Read Romans 12:1-2.

As you read this passage, focus on what Paul is saying. Use the space provided too brainstorm what you think this Scripture is saying.

- *What do you think the Spirit is trying to tell the church today?*
- *What does it mean to not be conformed to the pattern of the world?*
- *What kind of transformation (change) does God want to bring to our attitudes, interests, and personal agendas?*

Prayer: God, help me be conformed to your will and not to the world's. Amen.

Journal Page

The Life

Look Up
Matthew 22:37-40

[37]He replied, "You must love the Lord your God with all your heart, with all your being, and with all your mind. [38]This is the first and greatest commandment. [39]And the second is like it: You must love your neighbor as you love yourself. [40]All the Law and the Prophets depend on these two commands."

2 Corinthians 5:17-20

[17]So then, if anyone is in Christ, that person is part of the new creation. The old things have gone away, and look, new things have arrived!

[18]All of these new things are from God, who reconciled us to himself through Christ and who gave us the ministry of reconciliation. [19]In other words, God was reconciling the world to himself through Christ, by not counting people's sins against them. He has trusted us with this message of reconciliation.

[20]So we are ambassadors who represent Christ. God is negotiating with you through us. We beg you as Christ's representatives, "Be reconciled to God!"

Sum Up

Complete the following statements, and answer the question:

Loving God =

Loving people =

• *How will you play an active part in God's kingdom's growth?*

Wrap Up

- *Have you ever considered yourself a minister? Why, or why not?*

- *What do you feel is the hardest or scariest part of talking about Jesus to someone who doesn't know him?*

Lace Them Up

My backyard:

How I can minister in my backyard:

Day 1

Here I Am

Read Isaiah 6:1-8.

Imagine what you might have felt if you were Isaiah experiencing what he heard and saw. Use the space provided to reflect on your thoughts, especially about verse 5.

An invitation calls for an answer. When God calls and invites us into what God is doing, there is a need to respond.

- *What would you have done if you were in Isaiah's place? Why?*
- *What do you hear God calling you to now? What are some obstacles you face when deciding how to respond to God's invitation?*

Prayer: God, thank you for calling us all to ministry. Give us the strength to answer, "Here am I, Lord."

Journal Page

Longing

Read Psalm 42 slowly. During your first reading, come up with a word or a phrase that resonates with you. After you have read it a second time, focus on the images that the word or phrase you noticed brings to your mind. As you read this for the third time, reflect on what this psalm is saying to you.

- *What are the truths that this psalmist is trying to get across?*

Have you ever heard of the phrase "The Dark Night of the Soul"? This is phrase that is used when people are in a spiritual valley; and no matter what they do, they feel that they can't seem to get their footing. There are times in our lives where no matter where we go or what we do, we seemed to have lost God. We don't feel God's presence. These can be extremely agonizing and painful times, because we long for God.

The beauty is, however, that no matter what we are feeling, God is present. Even when our soul is longing for God and we can't feel him, God is present.

Prayer: God, thank you for never leaving our side. Amen.

Journal Page

Treasures

Read Matthew 6:19-21.

Use the space provided to reflect on what is most important to you. Write it in big letters or draw it large enough for you to look at it for a while. While you are reflecting on this object, read over this passage a few more times.

- *What do you want right now more than anything?*
- *What do you struggle with more than anything else right now?*

Jesus tells us that we should be careful of what we hold dear to our hearts.

- *What are some things that you see that are important to God?*
- *How are they important to you? How are they not important to you?*
- *How might the things that are important to God and God's kingdom become more important to you?*

Prayer: Holy God, thank you for accepting my burdens. Give me the strength to turn down worldly treasures and to stand for treasures that represent you. Amen.

Journal Page

Ambassadors

Read 2 Corinthians 5:16-21.

When we accept the love of God that was shown to us through Jesus Christ, we become something new. We become a new creation. Once we become this new creation, the way we once were is gone.

Use the space provided to reflect on the following questions:

- *What images come to your mind when you read this passage?*
- *What happens when someone is in Christ?*
- *How difficult or easy is this transition?*
- *What does it mean for you to be an ambassador of Christ?*

Prayer: God, "forgive us our trespasses as we forgive those who trespass against us." Amen.

Journal Page

Day 5

Take a Stand

Read John 8:1-11 several times. After you have read this passage several times, reflect on the following questions, keeping in mind that there will be times during our lives when we will be confronted with situations where injustices call for a response:

- *What images come to your mind when you read this Scripture?*
- *What, do you think, was Jesus writing in the sand?*
- *With whom do you most identify in the story?*
- *Based on Jesus' words and actions, describe the attitudes and actions he wants his followers to demonstrate?*

Prayer: Jesus, help me stand up for what is right, like you did. Help me live a life of love and compassion. Amen.

Journal Page

CPSIA information can be obtained
at www.ICGtesting.com
Printed in the USA
LVOW01s1730311015

460570LV00005B/6/P